Mother Less

Kim Gilpin

BookLeaf
Publishing

India | USA | UK

Presentation by *BookLeaf Publishing*

Web: www.bookleafpub.com

E-mail: info@bookleafpub.com

ISBN: 978-93-5744-456-9

First edition 2022

DEDICATION

To every girl/woman/person without a mom, whether you never had much of one to begin with, you lost the relationship with them at some point, or they moved on from this mortal realm, you are seen, you are loved, and I am proud of you. And to my Mom.

ACKNOWLEDGEMENT

This wouldn't have been written without my mother who was the inspiration, not just for this book but for the way I view and exist in the world. My mother was the most genuine person I have ever known, and I hope I inherited her reckless kindness and her belief that humanity can still be good (though some days that's harder than others). I carry her spirit with me wherever I go and hope one day we'll meet again in whatever way is possible.

When Does It Change?

When do little girls go from Mommy's little angel to spawn of Satan?

When do our mothers go from the center of our universe to the last person we want to be around?

When do we go from wanting to spend every moment together to barely being able to occupy the same room?

When does it change?
And when does it change back?

When do we grow up and realize our mother was just doing the best she could?

When does she remember what it's like to be a teenage girl just trying to make it through?

When do we make it through the storm and find our way back to one another?

Is this the normal progression of a mother and
daughter?

From adoration and love, to annoyance and
anger, and finally acceptance and admiration.

When does it change?

From daughter
to monster
to best friend

From mother
to tyrant
to trusted confidant

to gone

Shadow

Every day you dropped me off,
to Grandmother's house we go.

One of my earliest memories was being your
shadow.

You'd take me to the door and then I'd follow
you back to the car.

Trying to match your every footstep,
being your shadow.

Each step getting closer to the car that would
take you away,
another day a part.

Some days weren't as hard, I'd run back to
Grandma, and we'd wave as you drove away,
until we couldn't see you anymore.

Other days I'd cry and cry until you had to leave,
unable to wait for me to calm down.

All I wanted was to always be your shadow,
to follow in your footsteps everywhere you
went,
to never leave your side.

Was it as hard for you to leave me as it was for
me to let you go?

Grandparents

It wasn't bad though,
spending every day with my grandparents.

Far from it.

We played games and read books and went to
the library, took day trips and long drives in the
country just to get ice cream or play mini golf.

My grandparents were my favorite people.
I told them everything, things I wouldn't dream
of telling you.
I felt more at home in their home then I did in
our own.

It wasn't your fault, you had to work
and who better to watch me, nurture me, help me
grow and learn.

I remember imagining they were my parents
cause they were always there.

They didn't have to go to work, they had nothing
but time for me.

Even after I started school, I was there every
day.

They gave me a snack,
helped me with my homework,
watched me while I played,
did all the things my little brain assumed were
usually done by parents.

Little did I know how lucky I was,
to have them,
but also, you and dad.
Two full sets of adults who wanted nothing more
than for me to thrive and succeed.

But back then,
back then I just wanted more of your time.

And now,
now I can see you probably wanted the exact
same thing.

Florida (vacations)

There are so many pictures of our trip to Florida,
but I only remember bits and pieces.

I remember being surprised by my uncle,

closing my eyes through the entire Epcot ride,

spending more time off rides with dad,

long walks and hot sun,

begging for a Chip stuffed animal.

It was by far our biggest family vacation,
every kids dream,
but I barely remember it at all.

But what do I remember?

Weekends in the mountains or by the beach.

Trying to survive two hours alone in a hotel
room with my brother while
you and dad listened to the sales pitch.

Staying on a farm and watching a cow give
birth,
and the dog knocking the baby over time and
time again.

Me on rollerblades and everyone else on bikes
that I refused to learn to ride,
and skating into things to stop since I never
learned how to brake.

Mom calling my brother a "chicken shit" when
he wouldn't walk to the edge,
and laughing until my stomach hurt.

Swimming in lakes and ponds and oceans and
pools.

They weren't fancy or elaborate,
they weren't even that far from home,
and there aren't nearly as many pictures.

But they were special,
and some of my fondest memories with you.

Clothes

It started with clothes,
the beginning of the downfall.

I liked t-shirts and jeans, skater shoes and
oversized everything.
You liked dresses and blouses and a sensible flat.

I could wear what I wanted 6 days of the week,
but Sundays were for dresses.

And I hated it.

You only asked for one day
but it was still too much.

I whined,
and complained,
and cried,
and bitched,
and finally drove you crazy enough to say
FINE!
NO MORE DRESSES!

I know you didn't mean any harm,

you just wished you had a girl you could dress
up,
a girl who was a little more girlish.

I never told you the real reason I hated those
dresses,
how they just felt wrong,
how I didn't feel like myself,
how I couldn't quite put my finger on why they
made me feel so uncomfortable.

Maybe if I had you wouldn't have pushed so
hard for so long,
after all,
it's just clothes.

Sunday Morning

Sunday morning battles didn't end with dresses,
or bows,
or too tight shoes.

When I was little, I liked going to church.
Aside from dressing up, it was fun.
Listening to the children's lesson,
going to Sunday school with my friends,
and sometimes a treat afterwards.

But as I got older,
it lost its appeal.

Sitting blank faced in the choir loft,
next to you,
listening to a sermon and singing songs about
things I wasn't even sure I believed in,
and trying to stay awake through it all.

It became the newest rift,
the newest fight,
pulling me out of bed and to the car so we
wouldn't be late.

Your faith never wavered,
even as things got bleak,
mine however,
didn't just grow weak,
it broke completely.

Too many unanswered questions,
too many rules,
too many things I couldn't stand behind,
too much resentfulness and anger.

The fight stopped when I went to college,
you didn't even ask me to go on Christmas
anymore,
you just got dressed up and left without me.

And even though I didn't want to be there,
even though I didn't know what I believed in,
I still wish I had gone with you,
just to make you happy,
just to make you smile,
just to have a little more time.

The Anxiety Of It All

No one's to blame,
there just wasn't the information there is now,
no one to point it out,
what's a kid got to be anxious about anyway?

I couldn't make a decision to save my life,
no matter how many time limits,
or threats,
or pushing you did.

But I didn't know how to tell you why I couldn't
decide,
hell, I didn't know myself,
I just knew my chest got tight,
and my thoughts raced,
and how every little thing that could happen if I
made the wrong decision was whirling through
my mind.

You just thought I was being stubborn (I was
that too),
or that I was wasting time,

or that I was being defiant,
had I been able to describe it to you,
I know you would have understood.

Because years and years later,
we sat across a diner table,
and I told you how it felt,
how the panic would overtake me,
take my breath,
make me feel crazy and out of control.

And you cried with me,
and told me it would be ok,
and you'd help me in any way you could.

You weren't to blame,
we didn't know,
but I can't help but wonder how my life could
have been different,
if we did.

The Best Years of
Your Life (haha)

Everyone says you'll miss your youth,
and they're not wrong.
But to be a teenager again?
You couldn't pay me enough.

The panic attacks happened more and more,
especially at school,
middle school was hell,
always someone to give me a hard time,
I didn't tell you half the time,
I didn't think it would matter.

High school was only better because people left
me alone,
I still didn't have many friends,
but I'd rather be invisible then relentlessly
teased.
So, for that I was thankful.

But that doesn't mean it was fun,

or that there weren't days when boredom made
me a target,
I started getting sick every morning before I
went in,
the thought of the day ahead enough to make my
stomach churn to the point where I was running
to the bathroom every home room,
I was desperate for my teacher to ask what was
wrong,
they never did.

I didn't tell you,
it wasn't that I didn't think I could,
but you were busy,
and I didn't want to add to the that burden.

Plus, I didn't think you could possibly
understand,
what does a mom know about being a teenager?
We forget that parents once used to be in the
same place we are,
that they weren't always fully grown adults.
that the understand more than we know.

I never really asked you about high school,
did you like it?
were you popular or a reject like me?
did you get into trouble or keep your nose clean?

(I can probably guess that one, but you could
surprise me)

Kids never really think about their parents' life
before they existed,
the life they lived before we came along and
shook it all up,
I know countless stories of your childhood
but when it comes to your teens,
I draw a blank.

I wish I knew more,
I wish I could ask,
Not just about that but so many more things,
We always think there's more time,
I'll ask tomorrow,
Until tomorrow doesn't come.

Near or Far

I was going to reinvent myself in college,
that was the plan,
it didn't really work out that way.

But I did make a few friends,
and I did enjoy my classes,
and I did (eventually) find my place.

But at first,
I came home every single weekend,
calling you to come pick me up,
to drive an hour and a half each way
to pick me up and go right back home
and do it all again two days later.

But you never said no,
you were always there when I asked,
even though I'm sure it was a pain in the ass.

I remember getting sick the first time away from
home,
getting violently ill in the shared bathroom,
being the one to have to clean it up,
no one there to comfort me,

or take care.

I did at least wait until I thought you might be
awake,
and then I called,
tears falling,
you didn't hesitate,
didn't wait until after morning traffic,
just got in the car and came to get me.

I never forgot that.
It meant more than I think you knew.
It's not like I didn't know you would do anything
for me,
but that day you proved it,
that day you said you would always show up,
and you did.

Moving Out,
Moving On

The minute we didn't live together,
was the minute things changed,
in the best possible way.

Suddenly we could talk without it turning into
an argument,
Suddenly we had things in common,
shared interests and things to discuss,
Suddenly we could see eye to eye.

It was then I realized that we might have made it
to the other side,
that I could see who you really were,
instead of being blinded by teenage angst,
I was able to understand that maybe we weren't
all that different,
that actually we were more alike than I could
have ever imagined.

Had we finally turned the corner?
after years of turmoil,
after butting heads,

and screaming matches,
and slamming doors,
Had we finally gotten to the next level of our
relationship?

How come when you leave it gets easier?
When you want to spend more time together
is only after you're physically further away,
Maybe its true,
that distant makes the heart grow fonder.

Whatever the reason,
I was grateful,
to be able to see you in a new light,
and find in you the best friend I ever had.

New York, New York

One of the shared interests we found was theater,
we started taking trips to New York,
going to as many shows as we could,
staying in downtown hotels,
and taking in the sights of the city.

That was our time,
no one else was invited,
a weekend of just the two of us,
and I think we both savored every minute.

April 2019,
our last trip there,
you were sick the morning the bus was supposed
to leave,
it wasn't a rare occurrence at that point,
getting ill every morning,
though we didn't know why.

I took the bus by myself,
and you would meet me later.
And I enjoyed those few hours,

alone in the city,
getting a coffee,
and walking the busy streets by myself.

You did eventually come but something wasn't
right,
you barely ate the whole weekend,
and still would get sick,
you pushed on,
I'm sure mostly for me,
 and we still had a good time
but still something wasn't right.

It wouldn't be until months later,
that we found out exactly what was wrong.

Happy Birthday

June 12th, 2019.

How could I ever forget that day?

Your birthday.

And the day we found out.

Cancer.

Months of incorrect diagnoses.

Months of unanswered questions.

Months of maybe it's this, maybe it's that.

It could of been anything else, but it wasn't.

Cancer.

Happy fucking Birthday.

The Beginning (of the end)

The doctors seemed optimistic,
at least until they opened you up,
it was everywhere,
that's not an exaggeration,
that's what they said,
everywhere.

But there were still hopeful,
said treatment for this type of cancer was often
successful,
that there were options,
and plans,
and ways to stop the growth,
and destroy the cells,
and eventually go back in,
to take the rest out.

They said it so casually,
not that it's their fault,
they probably give this news 1000 times a year,
to 1000 different families,
and we were just one more.

It's not that they were bad doctors,
they weren't,
far from it,
some of the best,
but in the end,
they failed,
and it can't possibly hurt them as much as it hurt
us.

We didn't know then,
couldn't possibly know,
no matter how optimistic,
no matter how many plans,
no matter what they did,
we were at the beginning (of the end).

Hey Cancer...

Hey Cancer...
Fuck You.

July 2019.

After fighting for years,
after trying everything,
after all of it,
my aunt died.

We really believed she would make it,
she did too,
so did her doctors,
and then she was gone.

And I couldn't help but think,
were you next?
I sure you thought it too
but we didn't say anything.

Would cancer beat you too?
No, you'd beat it.
You had to.

Fighting (for your life)

You fought so hard,
from the very start,
your optimism was what kept you going,
even when things got hard.

But I know you struggled,
especially as weeks turned to months turned to a
year plus,
in and out of the hospital,
surgeries,
and tests,
and treatments,
chemo and radiation,
getting sick over and over again.

But you never let it show,
smiling through it all,
maybe it sounds cliché,
but that doesn't make it untrue.

I can't even imagine how difficult it was,
to fight for over two years,
to have three bad days for every good one,
and still you kept going,
thinking each new treatment would be the one to
fix it,
only to be disappointed again.

And then,
somehow,
someway,
you'd do it all over again.

(the beginning of)
The End

When you first told me,
I have to admit,
I was angry.

I didn't blame you,
I understood,
I knew why,
I totally got it,
but I was still angry,
hurt,
upset.

You were done,
you fought your fight,
you gave it all you could,
but you had nothing left,
and you were ready,
ready to go.

But I wasn't,
how could I ever be?

How could I ever be ready to say goodbye?

Couldn't you fight a little longer?
Try one more thing?
Give it one more shot?

But the doctors agreed,
it was time,
if you were ready,
they supported you.

And that was that.

I never told you how I felt,
I couldn't,
I didn't want you to know,
but I still felt guilty about it.

So, I supported your choice,
and pushed those feelings down,
but I wasn't ready,
I never could be.

Hospice

The walls were so white,
the halls so quiet,
family came in and out,
you seemed normal,
talking and laughing,
smiling and joking,
how were you dying?

When my grandmother was in hospice,
she wasn't even alert,
they just gave her pain meds for three days,
until she finally slipped away.

But you looked fine,
almost more healthy than you'd been in months,
it made it all seem even more unfair,
more cruel,
more difficult to understand.

White walls,
quiet halls,
it only got worse from there.

Home (Hospice)

Home is where everything changed,
from the first night,
you had already started going downhill.

How could I know?
How could I know that on that night when I
helped you into bed that you would never leave
that bed on your own volition again?
That the next time you would leave that room
would be when it was over.

Everything happened so quickly once you got
home,
that night you fell asleep and never fully woke
up again.

I wish I had one more real conversation with
you,
that I had stayed and talked to you a little longer,
that I had known,
but how could I have known?

The Last Three Days

Family came and went,

Did you eat?

Did you sleep?

Have you gotten any rest?

Yes.

Yes.

Yes.

True or not,
it didn't matter.

I spent a lot of time in your room,
watching you sleep,
watching your breathing,
watching your every twitch and move.

I felt robotic,
answering questions,
when you last had your meds,
reporting any new symptoms,
adjusting meds,
checking vitals.

After everyone left,
I sat next to you.

A sudden memory,
playing on the monkey bars,
hand after hesitant hand,
fingers slipped,
and I was on the ground,
hard on my back,
knocking the breath out of me,
it felt like this was it,
I couldn't breath,
I didn't know much but I knew that was
important.

In the blink of an eye,
there you were,
hand in mine,
reassuring words,
I looked at you,
and in an instant,
I knew I'd be ok,

if you said so,
than it had to be true.

I took your hand in mine,
I knew you didn't see me,
but I hoped you could hear me,
feel my hand in yours,
and hoped it brought you at least a small bit of
the comfort it brought me all those years ago.

Viewing/Funeral

Why is it always so damn hot?
As if the grief fills the room,
making it stiflingly warm.

So many people,
awkward hugs from this family member,
or that friend.

"I'm so sorry for your loss"

I know they mean it,
I truly do,
but it feels empty,
like its just what you're supposed to say.
I know,
I've said the same.

"This fucking sucks and it gonna suck for a long
time."

More truthful,
less appropriate.

Viewings and funerals were made for the living,
the dead don't know and they don't care.

But we do it anyway,
go through the motions,
cause that's how it's supposed to be.

If you ask me,
whoever came up with the idea,
was a fucking weirdo.

Mother Less

Two months.

Two months since I last heard your voice.

Two months since I last saw you.

Two months of this new reality.

Two months of this life without you.

I still think you'll answer the phone if I call,

that you'll be sitting in your chair when I walk
into your place,

that you'll be there.

How long until I forget the sound of your voice?

How long until I forget your laugh?

How long until I forget the feeling of your
presence?

There's no time limit on grief.

No rules on healing.

No way to know how I'll feel in another two
months, or two years or twenty years.

All I know is I miss you.

I miss your advice.

I miss your company.

I miss having my best friend, my confidant, my
sounding board.

I miss my mom.

There's no replacing you,

no coming back from this,

my new life,

of being Mother Less.